Dear Sophia,

Always believe in yourself
and everything will be possible
(like Nancy, who wanted to be a pilot).
Wishing you the very best on your
7ᵗʰ Birthday.
Much love from your best friend,
Nyrael   Sydney '16

Also in the *Meet . . .* series

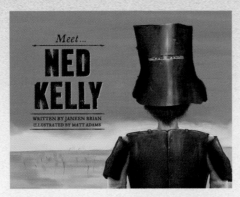

And look out for more *Meet . . .* books coming soon

Meet...
Nancy Bird Walton

WRITTEN BY GRACE ATWOOD
ILLUSTRATED BY HARRY SLAGHEKKE

RANDOM HOUSE AUSTRALIA

For Tarnia, my very special girl. HS

To Kes, who knows more about flying than a creature without wings should. GA

A Random House book
Published by Random House Australia Pty Ltd
Level 3, 100 Pacific Highway, North Sydney NSW 2060
www.randomhouse.com.au

First published by Random House Australia in 2014

Addresses for companies within the Random House Group can be found at www.randomhouse.com.au/offices

National Library of Australia
Cataloguing-in-Publication Entry

Author: Atwood, Grace
Title: Meet Nancy Bird Walton / Grace Atwood; Harry Slaghekke, illustrator
ISBN: 978 0 85798 387 9 (hbk)
Series: Meet; 6.
Target Audience: For children.
Subjects: Walton, Nancy Bird, 1915–2009 – Juvenile literature.
Women air pilots – Australia – Biography – Juvenile literature.
Other Authors/Contributors: Slaghekke, Harry, illustrator
Dewey Number: 629.13092

Quote on p. 6 from *Nancy Bird: Born to Fly* by Randal Flynn, illustrated by John Fairbridge, Macmillan Australia, Melbourne, 1991. Reproduced by permission of Macmillan Education Australia.

Quote on p. 22 from *My God! It's A Woman* by Nancy Bird Walton, Angus & Robertson, Sydney, 1990. Reproduced by kind permission of the Estate of the late Nancy Bird Walton.

Cover and internal design by Kirby Armstrong
Printed and bound in China by Everbest

Nancy Bird Walton grew up during the golden age of aviation. By the time she was 13, Nancy knew she wanted to fly.

This is the story of how Nancy began her career as Australia's first female commercial pilot.

Nancy Bird Walton attended her first flying lesson at Mascot in Sydney at the age of seventeen.

The famous aviator Charles Kingsford Smith was her instructor. Nancy's father didn't want her to be a pilot, but she was determined to follow her dream.

'My days went by in a sort of blur. I might have only 20 minutes in an aeroplane during the day, but I went out to the aerodrome every morning and stayed there until the fading light put a stop to flying for the day.'

Nancy knew there was more to learn than just how to fly a plane. She wanted to understand how and why planes could fly, so she spent as much time as she could at the flying school.

At first, the engineers gave Nancy basic jobs like scraping carbon off spark plugs. After she did those jobs without complaint, they taught her everything they knew about aircraft engines.

At last Nancy was ready to fly solo. She was terrified and didn't make it off the ground the first time. But a few days later, when her instructor suggested she try again, Nancy took a deep breath and decided to give it a go. Trembling with nerves, Nancy flew up into the air.

Nancy had to concentrate hard to remember everything she'd been taught.
It wasn't until she had landed that she could breathe a sigh of relief.

She had done it!

Nancy clocked up 100 hours of solo flying. She passed her exam and became the youngest woman in the British Empire to gain a commercial pilot's licence.

With help from her family, Nancy bought her first plane, a Gipsy Moth. She named it *Vincere*, which means 'to conquer' in Latin.

Nancy asked another female pilot, Peggy McKillop, to join her on an adventure around New South Wales. They would travel to country fairs and race meetings across the state, encouraging people to take an aeroplane ride they'd never forget.

On a crisp autumn day, Nancy and Peggy were ready for take-off. They flew out of Mascot and headed for Tamworth, leaving Sydney far behind.

The first ever 'Ladies Flying Tour' in Australia had begun.

To announce their arrival at the country fair, Nancy and Peggy circled the town several times in their small aircraft while an excited crowd gathered below to welcome the visiting pilots.

Peggy had many jobs as the co-pilot of *Vincere*. She had to swing the propeller to help start the engine, sell tickets and make sure each passenger got into the Gipsy Moth without putting their foot through the plane's fragile wing.

Sometimes it took a bit of convincing to get passengers to take a flight because it was still considered a dangerous and daredevil undertaking!

Nancy and Peggy continued on to Inverell, where they arrived on race day. The whole town had come to watch the horses, but Nancy stole the show by landing her Gipsy Moth in a paddock right beside the racecourse.

'I saw the vast great open spaces of this flat country. Huge artesian bore drains ran through the land like silver ribbons, and sheep by the thousands dotted the paddocks . . . Roly-poly grass raced before the wind, then piled high along the fence lines. Above all was the cloudless blue sky, stretching to the horizon.'

Navigation was particularly challenging for pilots in the 1930s. Nancy and Peggy used road maps, a compass and a watch to make sure they were heading in the right direction.

Landmarks such as powerlines and dams helped to guide them across rural New South Wales.

After more than 22,000 miles and lots of wonderful experiences, Nancy and Peggy returned to Sydney, exhausted but happy.

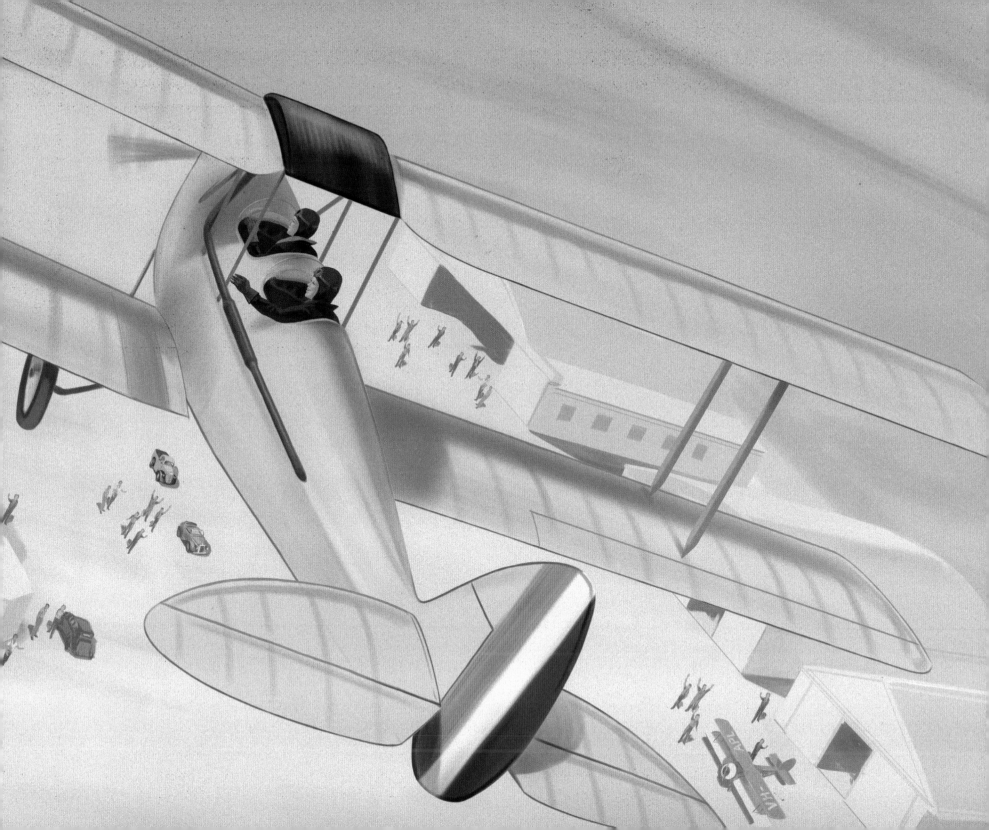

After the tour, Nancy met Reverend Stanley Drummond,
who ran the Far West Children's Health Scheme.

He asked her to go to Bourke and fly nurses out to remote areas
to help poor children in far western New South Wales.

The next exciting chapter in Nancy's life was about to begin.

TIMELINE

1915 (16 October): Nancy Bird Walton is born in Kew, New South Wales.

1933: Nancy has her first flying lesson, with Charles Kingsford Smith at Mascot, Sydney.

1935: Nancy receives her commercial pilot's licence, becoming the youngest woman in the British Empire to do so.

1935: Nancy buys her first aircraft, a Gipsy Moth she names *Vincere*, for £400.

1935: Peggy McKillop joins Nancy on their first barnstorming tour of New South Wales.

1935: Reverend Stanley Drummond of the Far West Children's Health Scheme hires Nancy to fly nurses to children in need of medical care in outback New South Wales. Nancy also transports patients requiring emergency treatment back to hospital, and becomes known as the 'Angel of the Outback'. This is the first time a female pilot has worked commercially in Australia.

1936: Nancy buys her second aircraft, a Leopard Moth. She starts picking up more commercial work and operating as an aerial ambulance service.

1936: Nancy wins the Ladies Trophy in the South Australian Centenary Air Race from Brisbane to Adelaide.

1939: Nancy marries Charles Walton. They will have two children.

1939–45: During World War II, Nancy recruits and trains women for an Australian women's auxiliary air force.

1950 (16 September): Nancy founds the Australian Women Pilots' Association with 34 other women pilots.

1958: Nancy enters the Powder Puff Derby, an air race across America for women pilots. She is the first overseas entry in the history of the race, and comes fifth.

1966 (11 June): Nancy is appointed an Officer of the Order of the British Empire.

1967: Nancy helps to establish the New South Wales Air Ambulance Service.

1990 (26 January): Nancy is awarded the Order of Australia.

1990: *My God! It's a Woman*, Nancy's memoir, is published.

2008 (30 September): Qantas names their first A380 fleet after Nancy.

2009 (13 January): Nancy dies, aged 93.